The Wonder of
WILD HORSES

To Dr. Jay F. Kirkpatrick and others like him, who have given so much
of themselves to make sure that wild horses will always have places to
roam wild and free.
— Mark Henckel

**For a free color catalog describing Gareth Stevens' list of high-quality books and
multimedia programs, call 1-800-542-2595 (USA) or 1-800-461-9120 (Canada).
Gareth Stevens Publishing's Fax: (414) 225-0377.
See our catalog, too, on the World Wide Web: http://gsinc.com**

Library of Congress Cataloging-in-Publication Data

Ritchie, Rita.
    The wonder of wild horses / by Rita Ritchie and Mark Henckel ; photographs by
Michael H. Francis ; illustrations by John F. McGee.
       p. cm. — (Animal wonders)
    Includes index.
    Summary: Text and illustrations provide an introduction to the wild horses that
still run free in the American West and on islands off the Atlantic coast.
    ISBN 0-8368-1563-7 (lib. bdg.)
    1. Wild horses—North America—Juvenile literature. [1. Wild horses. 2. Horses.]
I. Henckel, Mark. II. Francis, Michael H. (Michael Harlowe), 1953- ill.
III. McGee, John F., ill. IV. Title. V. Series.
SF360.3.N7R57   1996
599.72'5--dc20
                               96-5177

First published in North America in 1996 by
Gareth Stevens Publishing
1555 North RiverCenter Drive, Suite 201
Milwaukee, WI 53212 USA

This edition is based on the book *Wild Horse Magic for Kids* © 1995 by Mark Henckel, first
published in the United States in 1995 by NorthWord Press, Inc., Minocqua, Wisconsin, and
published in a library edition by Gareth Stevens, Inc., in 1995. All photographs © 1995 by
Michael H. Francis, with illustrations by John F. McGee. Additional end matter © 1996 by
Gareth Stevens, Inc.

Printed in the United States of America

1 2 3 4 5 6 7 8 9 99 98 97 96

The Wonder of
WILD HORSES

by Rita Ritchie and Mark Henckel
Photographs by Michael H. Francis
Illustrations by John F. McGee

Gareth Stevens Publishing
MILWAUKEE

The best place to meet a real cowboy or cowgirl or to see wild horses is in western areas of North America. There, herds of horses gallop wild and free. The first horses came to North America with European explorers about five hundred years ago.

Some of the horses eventually escaped or were turned loose. These horses became wild.

Wild horses learned to survive in rugged country under harsh conditions.

By the 1700s, millions of horses lived in North America, especially out West.

Wild horses
live as far west
as California,
as far north
as British
Columbia and
Alberta in
Canada, and
as far south
as Mexico.

Very few settlers saw the wild horses. But American Indians caught and tamed some of them.

Indian tribes living on the plains rode horses into battle and during bison hunts. Horses also carried the Indians and their belongings whenever the Indians moved.

Settlers came West to raise cattle and to farm. Most wild horses did not come near the farms. But sometimes, they broke down the fences and damaged crops.

The settlers caught some of the wild horses. They kept them for riding and farming. They also sold some of them to other settlers, to the army, and to the rodeo.

Today, most
wild horses
still live in
the West.
Some of them
also live on
islands off the
Atlantic coast.

Wild horses are gray, black, buckskin, or pinto in color. They eat any plants they can find, such as shrubs, trees, different kinds of grasses, and even poison ivy!

There used to be millions of wild horses. Now there are only about fifty thousand left.

Today, wild horses live in the dry hills. They share the land with mule deer and pronghorn antelope.

Most wild horses live in groups called harem bands. A band usually has five to seven horses — two or three females (mares), a male (stallion), and some year-lings. A mature mare leads the harem band.

The breed-
ing season
for wild
horses is
between
March
and July.
During
that time,
the stallion
is the
leader of
the band.

Young males live together in bachelor bands.

The stallion leader of a harem band has to fight off young males. Two horses bite and kick until one of them runs away. Old stallions have many scars.

Foals, or baby horses, are born each April and May. They live on their mother's milk at first. Soon, the new-born foals can run fast. They kick, jump, and run in circles.

Wild horses face great heat, cold, and drought. During drought, they paw the mud of dried-up  water holes to find water. The young, old, sick, or weak sometimes do not survive.

But most wild horses seem to
be hardy enough to survive
the extreme conditions.

Wild horses live in the open spaces of the West and on the islands off the Atlantic coast. If you use your imagination, you can almost see them racing with the wind.

Hopefully, rugged lands will always remain on Earth, so wild horses can continue to run free.

Glossary

bachelor band – a group of wild horses made up of young stallions without mares

breeding season – the time of year for reproducing, or producing offspring

buckskin – a horse that is yellow-brown in color, usually with a dark mane and tail

drought – a period of little or no rain

foal – a baby horse

harem band – a group of wild horses that includes a number of mares of different ages, a mature stallion, and yearlings

mare – a mature female horse

pinto – a spotted horse or pony

settlers – people from Europe who came to make their homes in North America not long after European explorers first arrived there

stallion – a mature male horse

yearlings – animals that are one year old or in the second year of life

Index